BASICS OF BITCOIN

PART OF OUR SERIES:

TOMORROW'S TECH: UNDERSTANDING THE BASICS

LIMITLESS PUBLISHING @ 2024

Table of Contents

Chapter 1: Introduction to Bitcoin 1
- History of Bitcoin 2
- Importance and relevance of Bitcoin in the modern financial landscape 3

Chapter 2: How Bitcoin Works 6
- Understanding blockchain technology 6
- Mining and validating transactions 8
- Public and Private keys, Wallets, and Addresses 10

Chapter 3: Buying and Storing Bitcoin 12
- Different methods to acquire Bitcoin (exchanges, ATMs, peer-to-peer) 12
- Secure storage options (hot wallets, cold storage, hardware wallets) 13
- Importance of private key security and best practices for storing Bitcoin 14

Chapter 4: Using Bitcoin for Transactions 17
- Sending and receiving Bitcoin payments 17
- Understanding transaction fees and confirmation times 18
- Real-world use cases of Bitcoin for purchases and payments 20

Chapter 5: Bitcoin Investment and Trading 22
- Different investment strategies for Bitcoin 22
- Risks and benefits of investing in Bitcoin 24
- Introduction to trading platforms and tools for trading Bitcoin 25

Chapter 6: Future of Bitcoin and Cryptocurrency 28
- Trends and developments in the cryptocurrency space 28
- Regulatory challenges and opportunities for Bitcoin 29
- Potential impact of Bitcoin on the global economy and financial systems 31

Conclusion: 33
- Recap of key concepts covered in the book 33
- Encouragement for further exploration and learning about Bitcoin 35
- Final thoughts on the transformative potential of Bitcoin 36

Chapter 1: Introduction to Bitcoin

Bitcoin is a groundbreaking digital currency that operates on a decentralized peer-to-peer network without the need for intermediaries such as banks or governments. It was created in 2009 by an unknown person or group of people using the pseudonym Satoshi Nakamoto. Bitcoin is often referred to as a cryptocurrency, as it uses cryptography to secure transactions, control the creation of new units, and verify the transfer of assets.

At its core, Bitcoin is a form of digital money that exists purely in electronic form. It is not physical like traditional currencies such as coins or banknotes. Instead, Bitcoin is stored in digital wallets, which are essentially software programs that allow users to send, receive, and store their bitcoins securely.

One of the key features of Bitcoin is its decentralized nature. Unlike traditional currencies that are issued and controlled by governments or central banks, Bitcoin operates on a decentralized network of computers known as nodes. These nodes work together to validate and record transactions on a public ledger called the blockchain.

The blockchain is a distributed and immutable ledger that contains a record of every Bitcoin transaction ever made. This transparency and immutability make it extremely difficult for anyone to manipulate or counterfeit transactions, ensuring the integrity and security of the Bitcoin network.

Another important aspect of Bitcoin is its limited supply. There will only ever be 21 million bitcoins in existence, a cap that is built into the code to control inflation and ensure scarcity. This scarcity is designed to increase the value of Bitcoin over time, making it a deflationary asset similar to gold.

Bitcoin can be used for a variety of purposes, including online purchases, remittances, investment, and as a store of value. Its borderless and censorship-resistant nature makes it particularly attractive for individuals looking to transact globally without the need for traditional financial institutions.

Overall, Bitcoin represents a paradigm shift in the world of finance, offering a decentralized alternative to traditional currencies and financial systems. Its underlying technology and principles have the potential to revolutionize the way we think about money and transactions in the digital age.

- History of Bitcoin

Bitcoin, the world's first decentralized cryptocurrency, was created by an unknown person or group of people using the pseudonym Satoshi Nakamoto. The concept of Bitcoin was first introduced in a whitepaper published in 2008 titled "Bitcoin: A Peer-to-Peer Electronic Cash System."

The actual implementation of Bitcoin took place in January 2009 when the first block of the Bitcoin blockchain, known as the Genesis Block, was mined by Satoshi Nakamoto. This marked the beginning of the Bitcoin network and the birth of a new era in digital currency.

In the early days, Bitcoin had little to no monetary value, and it was mainly used by cryptography enthusiasts and tech-savvy individuals. However, as more people started to recognize the potential of Bitcoin as a decentralized, secure, and censorship-resistant form of money, its popularity began to grow.

One of the significant milestones in the history of Bitcoin was the first real-world transaction involving the purchase of two pizzas for 10,000 bitcoins in May 2010. This event, now famously known as "Bitcoin Pizza Day," highlighted the early adoption of Bitcoin for everyday transactions.

Over the years, Bitcoin has experienced significant price volatility, with its value reaching new highs and enduring sharp corrections. Despite these fluctuations, Bitcoin has gained mainstream acceptance and has become a popular investment asset, attracting institutional investors and retail traders alike.

The creation of Bitcoin also paved the way for the development of thousands of other cryptocurrencies, collectively known as altcoins. These alternative cryptocurrencies aim to build upon the technology and principles introduced by Bitcoin while addressing its limitations and exploring new use cases.

As Bitcoin continues to evolve, its underlying technology, blockchain, has found applications beyond digital currencies, including supply chain management, voting systems, and smart contracts. The impact of Bitcoin on the financial landscape and the broader economy is still unfolding, with ongoing debates about its role in the future of money and finance.

In conclusion, the history of Bitcoin is a testament to the power of innovation and decentralization. From its humble beginnings to its current status as a global phenomenon, Bitcoin has revolutionized the way we think about money, technology, and trust. Its journey is far from over, and the future of Bitcoin promises to be as exciting and transformative as its past.

- Importance and relevance of Bitcoin in the modern financial landscape

Bitcoin, the pioneering cryptocurrency, has emerged as a significant player in the modern financial landscape, disrupting traditional financial systems and offering innovative solutions to various challenges. The importance and relevance of Bitcoin can be understood through several key aspects:

1. Decentralization and Financial Inclusion: Bitcoin operates on a decentralized network, free from control by any central authority. This decentralization empowers individuals to have direct control over their financial assets without

relying on intermediaries like banks. This is particularly crucial for the unbanked population globally, offering them access to financial services and opportunities that were previously unavailable.

2. Borderless Transactions: Bitcoin enables seamless and near-instantaneous transactions across borders without the need for traditional banking systems or currency conversion. This feature is especially beneficial for global trade and remittances, as it reduces costs and accelerates transaction speed, fostering greater economic efficiency.

3. Store of Value and Hedge Against Inflation: With a finite supply capped at 21 million coins, Bitcoin is often considered a digital store of value akin to digital gold. This characteristic makes it a popular choice for investors seeking to hedge against inflation and preserve the value of their assets in times of economic uncertainty.

4. Transparency and Security: The blockchain technology underlying Bitcoin ensures transparency and immutability of transactions, making it secure and resistant to fraud or tampering. This aspect enhances trust among users and eliminates the need for intermediaries to validate transactions, thereby reducing costs and enhancing security.

5. Financial Innovation and Technological Advancements: Bitcoin's emergence has paved the way for a host of financial innovations, such as smart contracts, decentralized finance (DeFi), and non-fungible tokens (NFTs). These advancements leverage blockchain technology to revolutionize various sectors beyond traditional finance, fostering a culture of innovation and disruption.

6. Challenges to Traditional Financial Systems: The rise of Bitcoin poses challenges to traditional financial systems and regulatory frameworks, prompting governments and financial institutions to reevaluate their approach to digital currencies and blockchain technology. This shift towards digital assets signifies a

broader transformation in the financial landscape, with Bitcoin at the forefront of this evolution.

In conclusion, Bitcoin's importance and relevance in the modern financial landscape are undeniable, with its disruptive potential reshaping traditional paradigms and paving the way for a more inclusive, efficient, and innovative financial ecosystem. Understanding and embracing the unique features of Bitcoin can empower individuals and institutions to harness the benefits of this transformative technology for a more sustainable and equitable financial future.

Chapter 2: How Bitcoin Works

- Understanding blockchain technology

Blockchain technology is the underlying technology behind cryptocurrencies like Bitcoin. It is a decentralized and distributed ledger that records transactions across a network of computers. This technology is considered revolutionary because it allows for secure, transparent, and immutable record-keeping without the need for a central authority.

Key Concepts of Blockchain Technology:

1. Decentralization: One of the key features of blockchain technology is decentralization. This means that there is no central authority controlling the network. Instead, transactions are validated by a network of computers (nodes) that work together to maintain the integrity of the blockchain.

2. Distributed Ledger: The blockchain is a distributed ledger, meaning that a copy of the entire ledger is maintained on each node in the network. This ensures that there is no single point of failure and that the data is secure and tamper-proof.

3. Blocks and Chains: The blockchain is made up of blocks, which contain a list of transactions. Each block is linked to the previous block, forming a chain of blocks. This chain of blocks is what gives the technology its name - blockchain.

4. Consensus Mechanisms: In order to add a new block to the blockchain, the network of nodes must come to a consensus on the validity of the transactions in that block. There are different consensus mechanisms, such as Proof of Work (used by Bitcoin) and Proof of Stake, which determine how consensus is reached.

5. Immutability: Once a block is added to the blockchain, it is considered immutable, meaning that it cannot be altered or deleted. This ensures the integrity of the data and prevents fraud or tampering.

6. Transparency: The blockchain is a transparent technology, as all transactions are recorded on the ledger and can be viewed by anyone with access to the network. This transparency helps to build trust among users and ensures accountability.

Applications of Blockchain Technology:

1. Cryptocurrencies: The most well-known application of blockchain technology is in the creation and use of cryptocurrencies like Bitcoin. Blockchain technology enables secure and transparent transactions without the need for a central authority.

2. Smart Contracts: Blockchain technology can also be used to create and execute smart contracts, which are self-executing contracts with the terms of the agreement written into code. This eliminates the need for intermediaries and automates the execution of contracts.

3. Supply Chain Management: Blockchain technology can be used to track and trace products throughout the supply chain, ensuring transparency and authenticity. This can help to reduce fraud, improve efficiency, and enhance trust among participants.

4. Voting Systems: Blockchain technology can be used to create secure and transparent voting systems, ensuring the integrity of the voting process and preventing fraud.

In conclusion, blockchain technology is a revolutionary technology that has the potential to disrupt many industries and change the way we transact and interact online. By understanding the key concepts and applications of blockchain technology, individuals can better appreciate its benefits and possibilities for the future.

- Mining and validating transactions

Mining and validating transactions are essential components of the Bitcoin network that ensure the security, integrity, and decentralization of the system. In this section, we will delve into the intricacies of mining and how transactions are verified on the Bitcoin network.

Mining Process:

Mining is the process by which new transactions are added to the public ledger known as the blockchain. Miners are individuals or groups of people who use powerful computers to solve complex mathematical puzzles. These puzzles are crucial in validating and securing new transactions on the network.

When a transaction is initiated on the Bitcoin network, it is grouped with other pending transactions into a block. Miners compete to solve the mathematical puzzle associated with the block. The first miner to solve the puzzle broadcasts the solution to the network, and the block is added to the blockchain.

Validation of Transactions:

Validating transactions is a crucial part of the mining process. When a miner successfully solves the mathematical puzzle and adds a block to the blockchain, all the transactions within that block are considered validated. This means that the transactions are legitimate and have been approved by the network.

To validate a transaction, miners must ensure that the sender has sufficient funds to complete the transaction and that the transaction meets all the necessary criteria. Once a transaction is validated, it is irreversible and becomes a permanent part of the blockchain.

Incentives for Miners:

Miners are incentivized to participate in the mining process through the reward system built into the Bitcoin protocol. When a miner successfully adds a new block to the blockchain, they are rewarded with a certain number of newly minted bitcoins. This reward serves as an incentive for miners to dedicate their time and resources to securing the network.

In addition to the block reward, miners also receive transaction fees for validating transactions. Users can choose to attach a fee to their transactions to prioritize them for validation by miners. This fee is collected by the miner who successfully includes the transaction in a block.

Conclusion:

Mining and validating transactions are vital functions that underpin the Bitcoin network. By participating in the mining process, individuals help maintain the security and integrity of the blockchain. Through a combination of computational power, consensus mechanisms, and incentives, the Bitcoin network continues to operate as a decentralized and secure system for peer-to-peer transactions.

- Public and Private keys, Wallets, and Addresses

In the world of Bitcoin and other cryptocurrencies, public and private keys play a crucial role in securing your digital assets. Understanding how these keys work, along with wallets and addresses, is essential for anyone looking to engage in cryptocurrency transactions.

1. Public and Private Keys:
- Public Key: Your public key is a unique alphanumeric string that acts as your wallet address. It is used to receive funds from other users on the blockchain. The public key is derived from the private key through a complex mathematical algorithm, but it cannot be used to reverse-engineer the private key.
- Private Key: Your private key is a secret code that allows you to access and control your cryptocurrency funds. It is essential to keep your private key secure and never share it with anyone, as anyone with access to your private key can manipulate your funds.

2. Wallets:
- A cryptocurrency wallet is a digital tool that allows you to securely store, send, and receive your digital assets. Wallets can come in various forms, including software wallets, hardware wallets, paper wallets, and online wallets.
- Software Wallets: These are applications that you can install on your computer or mobile device. They are convenient to use but are susceptible to hacking if your device is compromised.
- Hardware Wallets: These are physical devices that store your private keys offline, offering a high level of security against online threats. Hardware wallets are considered one of the safest ways to store cryptocurrencies.
- Paper Wallets: A paper wallet is a physical document containing your public and private keys. It is an offline method of storing your keys, making it immune to cyberattacks. However, paper wallets can be easily lost or damaged if not

stored properly.
- Online Wallets: These are wallets provided by cryptocurrency exchanges or online platforms. While convenient for trading, online wallets are considered less secure compared to hardware or paper wallets due to the risk of hacking.

3. Addresses:
- A cryptocurrency address is a unique identifier derived from your public key. It is used to receive funds from other users and serves as a destination for sending cryptocurrencies. Each cryptocurrency has its own address format, so it is crucial to use the correct address when sending or receiving funds.
- Addresses are case-sensitive and consist of a combination of letters and numbers. It is recommended to double-check the recipient's address before sending any funds to avoid irreversible mistakes.
- It is important to note that your public address is safe to share with others, as it only allows users to send funds to your wallet. On the other hand, your private key should always remain confidential to prevent unauthorized access to your funds.

In conclusion, understanding the concepts of public and private keys, wallets, and addresses is essential for safely managing your cryptocurrency holdings. By following best practices for securing your keys and using reputable wallets, you can protect your digital assets from potential threats and enjoy a secure cryptocurrency experience.

Chapter 3: Buying and Storing Bitcoin

- Different methods to acquire Bitcoin (exchanges, ATMs, peer-to-peer)

Acquiring Bitcoin can be done through various methods, each offering its own advantages and considerations. The most common methods include exchanges, ATMs, and peer-to-peer transactions.

1. Exchanges
- Centralized Exchanges: These platforms facilitate the buying and selling of Bitcoin using traditional currencies. Users create an account, deposit funds, and place buy or sell orders.
- Decentralized Exchanges (DEX): DEX platforms allow users to trade directly with each other without a central authority. Users retain control of their funds throughout the trading process.
- Considerations: Exchanges may vary in terms of fees, security measures, liquidity, and user-friendliness. It is important to choose a reputable exchange with a good track record to ensure the safety of your investments.

2. ATMs
- Bitcoin ATMs: These machines allow users to buy Bitcoin using cash or debit/credit cards. Users can locate Bitcoin ATMs in public places like malls, airports, and convenience stores.
- Process: Users can initiate a purchase by entering the amount they wish to buy and providing a Bitcoin wallet address. The machine then dispenses the equivalent amount of Bitcoin to the user's wallet.
- Considerations: Bitcoin ATMs may charge higher fees compared to online exchanges. Users should also consider the machine's security features and reputation before making a transaction.

3. Peer-to-Peer Transactions

- Marketplaces: Platforms like LocalBitcoins and Paxful connect buyers and sellers directly for peer-to-peer transactions. Users can negotiate prices, payment methods, and terms of the trade.
- Considerations: Peer-to-peer transactions offer more privacy and flexibility compared to centralized exchanges. However, users should exercise caution and verify the reputation of the counterparty before conducting a trade.

 Conclusion

Acquiring Bitcoin through exchanges, ATMs, or peer-to-peer transactions provides users with various options to enter the cryptocurrency market. Each method comes with its own set of advantages and considerations, so it is important for users to conduct thorough research and choose a method that aligns with their preferences and risk tolerance. Remember to always prioritize security and use reputable platforms when acquiring Bitcoin.

- Secure storage options (hot wallets, cold storage, hardware wallets)

Secure storage options are crucial when it comes to managing bitcoins and other cryptocurrencies

1. Hot Wallets:

Hot wallets are software-based wallets that are connected to the internet. They are convenient for frequent transactions and easy access to funds. However, hot wallets are more vulnerable to hacking and security breaches since they are online. Examples of hot wallets include online wallets, mobile wallets, and desktop wallets. Users should exercise caution when using hot wallets and ensure that they have strong security measures in place, such as two-factor authentication and regular software updates.

2. Cold Storage:

Cold storage refers to storing bitcoins offline, which greatly reduces the risk of hacking and cyber attacks. Cold storage options include paper wallets and hardware wallets. Paper wallets involve printing out the public and private keys on a piece of paper and storing it securely. While paper wallets are secure, they are not user-friendly for regular transactions. Hardware wallets, on the other hand, are physical devices that store private keys offline. They provide a high level of security and are convenient for both storage and transactions.

3. Hardware Wallets:
Hardware wallets are considered one of the most secure storage options for bitcoins. These are physical devices designed to securely store private keys offline, away from potential online threats. Hardware wallets are immune to computer viruses and malware, making them ideal for long-term storage of large amounts of bitcoins. Popular hardware wallet brands include Ledger, Trezor, and KeepKey. Users need to set up a hardware wallet by creating a secure PIN code and backing up the recovery seed phrase. Hardware wallets are convenient, user-friendly, and provide a high level of security for managing bitcoins.

- Importance of private key security and best practices for storing Bitcoin

In the world of Bitcoin and cryptocurrencies, private key security is of utmost importance. A private key is a sophisticated form of cryptography that allows users to access their funds and conduct transactions on the Bitcoin network. If a private key is compromised or lost, the associated Bitcoin funds can be irreversibly lost as well. Here are some key points highlighting the importance of private key security and best practices for storing Bitcoin:

1. Control Your Private Keys: The first and most crucial step in ensuring the security of your Bitcoin holdings is to have control over your private keys. This means storing your Bitcoin in a wallet where you are the sole owner of the private keys, such as a hardware wallet or a non-custodial software wallet.

2. Use Hardware Wallets: Hardware wallets are physical devices that store your

private keys offline, providing an extra layer of security against hacking and malware attacks. They are considered one of the safest ways to store Bitcoin for long-term holdings.

3. Backup Your Private Keys: It is essential to create secure backups of your private keys to prevent the risk of losing access to your funds in case of device failure or loss. Backup methods include writing down seed phrases on paper and storing them in a secure location, or using encrypted USB drives.

4. Protect Your Seed Phrase: The seed phrase, also known as a recovery phrase, is a list of words that can be used to restore access to your Bitcoin wallet in case your device is lost or damaged. It is crucial to keep your seed phrase secure and private, as anyone with access to it can potentially steal your funds.

5. Avoid Storing Private Keys Online: Storing private keys on online platforms or in cloud storage exposes them to the risk of hacking and theft. It is recommended to keep your private keys offline and away from internet-connected devices to minimize the risk of unauthorized access.

6. Use Multisig Wallets: Multisig wallets require multiple private keys to authorize a transaction, adding an extra layer of security by distributing control among multiple parties. This can help protect your funds in case one of the private keys is compromised.

7. Regularly Update Your Wallet Software: Keeping your wallet software up to date is important to ensure that you have the latest security features and patches for any potential vulnerabilities. Always download wallet software from official sources to avoid downloading malicious software.

By following these best practices for storing Bitcoin and securing your private keys, you can minimize the risk of losing your funds to theft, hacking, or other security threats. Remember, the security of your private keys is paramount in the world of Bitcoin, and taking proactive measures to protect them is essential for safeguarding your cryptocurrency holdings.

Chapter 4: Using Bitcoin for Transactions

- Sending and receiving Bitcoin payments

Bitcoin, the revolutionary decentralized digital currency, allows users to send and receive payments in a peer-to-peer manner without the need for intermediaries like banks. Understanding how to send and receive Bitcoin payments is fundamental to utilizing this innovative financial system effectively.

Sending Bitcoin Payments:
To send Bitcoin to someone, you need their Bitcoin address. A Bitcoin address is a unique string of alphanumeric characters that acts as a destination for the funds. Here is a step-by-step guide on how to send Bitcoin payments:
1. Obtain the recipient's Bitcoin address: The recipient should provide you with their Bitcoin address, which you can copy and paste or scan using a QR code.
2. Access your Bitcoin wallet: You need a Bitcoin wallet to send funds. Open your wallet and navigate to the send or transfer section.
3. Enter the recipient's Bitcoin address: Paste the recipient's Bitcoin address in the designated field. Double-check the address to ensure it is correct since transactions on the Bitcoin network are irreversible.
4. Specify the amount: Enter the amount of Bitcoin you wish to send. Some wallets also allow you to select the transaction fee based on the speed of confirmation you desire.
5. Confirm the transaction: Review the transaction details, including the recipient's address and the amount, before confirming the payment. Once you confirm the transaction, it will be broadcast to the Bitcoin network for verification and inclusion in a block.

Receiving Bitcoin Payments:
Receiving Bitcoin payments is a straightforward process that involves sharing your Bitcoin address with the sender. Follow these steps to receive Bitcoin

payments:

1. Share your Bitcoin address: Provide your Bitcoin address to the person who intends to send you funds. You can display your address as a QR code for easy scanning.
2. Wait for the transaction: Once the sender initiates the transaction, it will be broadcast to the Bitcoin network for validation. Transactions typically take a few minutes to be confirmed, but this can vary based on network congestion and the transaction fee paid.
3. Check your wallet: After the transaction is confirmed and included in a block, you will see the received Bitcoin in your wallet balance. It is recommended to wait for multiple confirmations to ensure the transaction's security.

Conclusion:

Sending and receiving Bitcoin payments is a fundamental aspect of utilizing Bitcoin as a digital currency. Understanding the process of sending and receiving payments ensures smooth and secure transactions within the decentralized network. By following the steps outlined above and exercising caution when sharing addresses or confirming transactions, users can navigate the world of Bitcoin payments with confidence and ease.

- Understanding transaction fees and confirmation times

One of the key aspects of using Bitcoin is understanding transaction fees and confirmation times. These two factors play a crucial role in the efficiency, security, and cost of sending and receiving Bitcoin transactions.

1. Transaction Fees:
Transaction fees are charges paid by users to miners to prioritize their transactions on the Bitcoin network. These fees are essential for incentivizing miners to include transactions in the next block and secure the network. The amount of transaction fee you choose to attach to your transaction determines

how quickly it will be processed by miners.

- Importance of Transaction Fees: Transaction fees ensure that miners have an incentive to validate and include your transaction in a block. Without transaction fees, miners may prioritize transactions with higher fees, leading to delays in processing your transaction.
- Calculating Transaction Fees: Transaction fees are calculated based on the size of the transaction in bytes and the current network congestion. Wallets usually provide fee estimation tools to help users choose an appropriate fee for their transactions.
- Dynamic Fee Structure: Transaction fees are not fixed and can vary depending on network conditions. During times of high congestion, fees may increase to prioritize transactions with higher fees.

2. Confirmation Times:
Confirmation time refers to the time it takes for a transaction to be included in a block and added to the Bitcoin blockchain. The number of confirmations a transaction receives indicates the level of security and finality of the transaction.

- Importance of Confirmation Times: Confirmations provide security against double-spending attacks and ensure that transactions are irreversible once they are included in a block.
- Factors Affecting Confirmation Times: Confirmation times can vary depending on network congestion, transaction fees, block size limits, and the mining power of the network. Higher transaction fees generally lead to faster confirmation times.
- Waiting for Confirmations: It is recommended to wait for multiple confirmations (usually 6 confirmations) to ensure that a transaction is secure and immutable. However, for low-value transactions, a few confirmations may be sufficient.

In conclusion, understanding transaction fees and confirmation times is essential for effectively using Bitcoin. By choosing appropriate transaction fees and being patient with confirmation times, users can ensure the security and efficiency of their Bitcoin transactions.

- **Real-world use cases of Bitcoin for purchases and payments**

Bitcoin, the world's first decentralized digital currency, has gained popularity not only as a store of value but also as a means of making purchases and payments in the real world. Here are some key use cases where Bitcoin is being actively used for transactions:

1. Online Retailers: Many online retailers now accept Bitcoin as a form of payment. Major e-commerce platforms such as Overstock, Newegg, and Shopify allow customers to pay for products using Bitcoin. This is particularly useful for international transactions, as Bitcoin eliminates the need to convert currencies and can facilitate quick and secure cross-border payments.

2. Travel and Accommodation: Some travel agencies and hotel booking platforms now accept Bitcoin for booking flights, hotels, and other travel-related services. This allows travelers to avoid traditional banking fees and exchange rate costs when making international bookings.

3. Gift Cards and Vouchers: Various platforms offer gift cards and vouchers that can be purchased with Bitcoin. This enables users to buy gift cards for popular retailers and services using their Bitcoin holdings, expanding the utility of the cryptocurrency beyond direct purchases.

4. Charitable Donations: Bitcoin has been used for charitable donations to various organizations and causes. Non-profit organizations often accept Bitcoin donations due to its transparency, low transaction fees, and ease of cross-border transfers. This allows donors to contribute to causes they care about using

cryptocurrency.

5. Remittances: Bitcoin is increasingly being used for international remittances, especially in regions with limited access to traditional banking services. By using Bitcoin, individuals can send money across borders quickly and at a lower cost compared to traditional remittance services.

6. Peer-to-Peer Transactions: Bitcoin's peer-to-peer nature allows individuals to transact directly with one another without the need for intermediaries. This has led to the rise of Bitcoin marketplaces where users can buy and sell goods and services directly using Bitcoin.

7. Subscription Services: Some subscription-based services, such as streaming platforms, VPN providers, and online publications, now accept Bitcoin as a payment option. Subscribers can pay for their monthly or annual subscriptions using Bitcoin, offering an alternative payment method to traditional credit cards or PayPal.

Overall, Bitcoin's use cases for purchases and payments continue to expand as more merchants and service providers adopt the cryptocurrency. With its fast transactions, low fees, and borderless nature, Bitcoin offers a convenient and secure way to make transactions in the digital age.

Chapter 5: Bitcoin Investment and Trading

- Different investment strategies for Bitcoin

Investing in Bitcoin can be a rewarding venture, but it also comes with its own set of risks and challenges. To make informed decisions when investing in Bitcoin, it's essential to understand and consider various investment strategies. Here are some popular strategies that investors often employ:

1. HODLing (Hold on for Dear Life):
   HODLing is a long-term investment strategy where investors buy Bitcoin and hold onto it for an extended period, regardless of short-term market fluctuations. This strategy is based on the belief that Bitcoin's value will increase over time due to its scarcity and growing adoption.

2. Dollar-Cost Averaging (DCA):
   Dollar-cost averaging involves investing a fixed amount of money in Bitcoin at regular intervals, regardless of the current price. By spreading out purchases over time, investors can mitigate the impact of price volatility and potentially lower their average cost per Bitcoin.

3. Swing Trading:
   Swing trading involves buying Bitcoin when the price is expected to rise and selling when the price is expected to drop. This strategy requires active monitoring of the market and making frequent trades to capitalize on short-term price movements.

4. Day Trading:
   Day trading is a high-risk, high-reward strategy that involves buying and selling Bitcoin within the same day to profit from short-term price fluctuations. Day traders often rely on technical analysis and market trends to make quick trading

decisions.

5. Arbitrage:

Arbitrage involves exploiting price differences of Bitcoin across different exchanges or markets to make a profit. This strategy requires quick execution and close monitoring of price variations to capitalize on arbitrage opportunities.

6. Bitcoin Lending:

Bitcoin lending involves lending out your Bitcoin to earn interest or fees from borrowers. This strategy allows investors to earn passive income on their Bitcoin holdings but comes with risks such as default by borrowers or platform insolvency.

7. Bitcoin Mining:

Bitcoin mining is the process of validating transactions on the Bitcoin network and securing the network by solving complex mathematical puzzles. Miners are rewarded with newly minted Bitcoins and transaction fees. This strategy requires significant upfront investment in mining equipment and electricity costs.

8. Portfolio Diversification:

Diversifying your investment portfolio by including Bitcoin alongside traditional assets like stocks, bonds, and real estate can help spread risk and potentially increase returns. This strategy allows investors to benefit from Bitcoin's potential upside while mitigating the risks associated with a single asset class.

It's important to note that each investment strategy comes with its own set of risks and rewards, and what works for one investor may not work for another. Before choosing a strategy, investors should conduct thorough research, consider their risk tolerance and investment goals, and seek advice from financial professionals if needed.

- Risks and benefits of investing in Bitcoin

Investing in Bitcoin, like any other financial endeavor, comes with its own set of risks and benefits. It is important for potential investors to weigh these factors carefully before deciding to invest in this volatile digital currency.

Risks:

1. Volatility: Bitcoin is known for its extreme price fluctuations. The value of Bitcoin can rise or fall rapidly within a short period of time, making it a highly volatile investment. This volatility can result in significant gains or losses for investors.

2. Regulatory Risks: The regulatory environment surrounding Bitcoin is still evolving, and changes in regulations could impact the value and legality of Bitcoin investments. Government crackdowns or restrictions on Bitcoin could have a negative impact on its value.

3. Security Risks: Bitcoin transactions are irreversible, and once a transaction is made, it cannot be undone. This makes Bitcoin susceptible to hacking, theft, and fraud. Investors need to take precautions to secure their Bitcoin holdings, such as using secure wallets and following best security practices.

4. Market Risks: The cryptocurrency market is relatively young and can be influenced by market manipulation, speculation, and other factors that may not be present in traditional financial markets. Investors should be prepared for sudden market shifts and be aware of the risks involved.

Benefits:

1. Decentralization: Bitcoin operates on a decentralized network, meaning that it is not controlled by any single entity, such as a government or financial institution. This decentralization offers users greater control over their funds and financial transactions.

2. Potential for High Returns: Despite its volatility, Bitcoin has shown the potential for high returns over the years. Many early investors in Bitcoin have seen significant gains, and some believe that the price of Bitcoin could continue to rise in the future.

3. Diversification: Adding Bitcoin to an investment portfolio can provide diversification benefits, as it is not directly correlated with traditional asset classes like stocks and bonds. Including Bitcoin in a portfolio can help spread risk and potentially improve overall returns.

4. Global Accessibility: Bitcoin can be accessed and used by anyone with an internet connection, regardless of their location or background. This global accessibility makes Bitcoin an attractive investment option for individuals looking to participate in the digital economy.

In conclusion, investing in Bitcoin can be a high-risk, high-reward proposition. Potential investors should carefully consider the risks and benefits outlined above before deciding to invest in this digital currency. It is advisable to conduct thorough research, seek professional advice, and only invest what you can afford to lose.

- Introduction to trading platforms and tools for trading Bitcoin

Trading Bitcoin has become increasingly popular as more people are interested in investing in cryptocurrencies. To effectively trade Bitcoin, it is important to understand the various trading platforms and tools available to traders. In this section, we will explore the basics of trading platforms and the tools that can help you navigate the world of Bitcoin trading.

1. Trading Platforms:
Trading platforms are online marketplaces where buyers and sellers can trade Bitcoin and other cryptocurrencies. These platforms act as intermediaries, connecting buyers and sellers and facilitating the exchange of digital assets. Some popular trading platforms for Bitcoin include Coinbase, Binance, Kraken, and Bitfinex.

- Coinbase: Coinbase is one of the most user-friendly platforms for beginners. It allows users to buy, sell, and store Bitcoin easily. Coinbase also offers a mobile app for convenient trading on the go.

- Binance: Binance is known for its wide range of cryptocurrencies available for trading. It has advanced trading features such as margin trading and futures trading, making it suitable for more experienced traders.

- Kraken: Kraken is a well-established exchange with a strong reputation for security and reliability. It offers a variety of trading pairs and advanced order types, making it a popular choice for serious traders.

- Bitfinex: Bitfinex is known for its liquidity and advanced trading features. It offers margin trading, lending, and a wide range of trading pairs, making it suitable for traders looking for more flexibility.

2. Tools for Trading Bitcoin:
In addition to trading platforms, there are various tools that can help traders analyze the market, make informed decisions, and execute trades more effectively. Some essential tools for trading Bitcoin include:

- Price Charts: Price charts provide a visual representation of the price movement of Bitcoin over time. Traders use price charts to identify trends, support and resistance levels, and potential entry and exit points for trades.

- Technical Analysis Indicators: Technical analysis indicators, such as moving averages, relative strength index (RSI), and MACD, help traders analyze price movements and identify potential trading opportunities based on historical price data.

- Order Book: The order book shows the current buy and sell orders for Bitcoin on a trading platform. Traders use the order book to assess market depth, liquidity, and potential price movements.

- Trading Bot: Trading bots are automated software programs that execute trades on behalf of traders based on predefined criteria. Trading bots can help traders take advantage of opportunities in the market and execute trades more efficiently.

In conclusion, trading Bitcoin requires a good understanding of trading platforms and tools to navigate the volatile cryptocurrency market successfully. By using the right platforms and tools, traders can make informed decisions, manage risks effectively, and optimize their trading strategies for better results.

Chapter 6: Future of Bitcoin and Cryptocurrency

- Trends and developments in the cryptocurrency space

The world of cryptocurrency is a fast-evolving ecosystem, with new trends and developments constantly shaping the industry. In this section, we will explore some of the key trends and developments that are currently influencing the cryptocurrency space.

1. Institutional Adoption: One of the most significant trends in the cryptocurrency space is the increasing interest and adoption by institutional investors. Large financial institutions, hedge funds, and corporations are beginning to invest in cryptocurrencies, driving up demand and legitimizing the asset class. This trend is expected to continue as more institutional players enter the market.

2. Regulatory Environment: Another important trend in the cryptocurrency space is the evolving regulatory environment. Governments around the world are starting to implement regulations to govern the use of cryptocurrencies, exchanges, and initial coin offerings (ICOs). This regulatory clarity is crucial for the long-term sustainability and mainstream adoption of cryptocurrencies.

3. Stablecoins: Stablecoins have emerged as a popular trend in the cryptocurrency space, offering a digital asset pegged to a stable fiat currency like the US dollar. These stablecoins provide a way for users to transact in a more stable currency while still benefiting from the advantages of blockchain technology.

4. DeFi (Decentralized Finance): DeFi has been a major development in the cryptocurrency space, offering a range of financial services such as lending, borrowing, and trading without the need for traditional intermediaries. DeFi platforms are built on blockchain technology and smart contracts, enabling a

more open and accessible financial system.

5. NFTs (Non-Fungible Tokens): NFTs have gained significant attention in the cryptocurrency space, allowing for the creation and ownership of unique digital assets. These tokens are used for a variety of purposes, including digital art, collectibles, and in-game assets. The NFT market has seen explosive growth, attracting artists, creators, and investors alike.

6. Scalability Solutions: Scalability remains a key challenge for many blockchain networks, with issues like high transaction fees and slow confirmation times hindering mainstream adoption. Various scalability solutions, such as layer 2 protocols and sharding, are being developed to address these challenges and improve the efficiency of blockchain networks.

7. Environmental Concerns: The environmental impact of cryptocurrency mining has become a significant issue in the industry. The energy consumption of Bitcoin and other proof-of-work cryptocurrencies has raised concerns about sustainability and carbon emissions. As a result, there is a growing focus on developing more energy-efficient consensus mechanisms and promoting sustainable mining practices.

Overall, the cryptocurrency space continues to evolve at a rapid pace, with new trends and developments shaping the industry's future. As the ecosystem matures and innovations continue to emerge, it is essential for participants to stay informed and adapt to these changes to navigate the dynamic landscape of cryptocurrencies effectively.

- Regulatory challenges and opportunities for Bitcoin

As Bitcoin and other cryptocurrencies continue to gain popularity and acceptance in the financial world, regulatory challenges have emerged as a significant issue that needs to be addressed. The decentralized and borderless nature of Bitcoin presents unique challenges for regulators around the world. At the same time, these challenges also present opportunities for innovation and growth in the financial sector.

Challenges:

1. Lack of Regulatory Clarity: One of the major challenges facing Bitcoin is the lack of consistent and clear regulatory framework across different jurisdictions. This creates uncertainty for businesses and consumers, leading to potential legal risks and barriers to adoption.

2. Money Laundering and Terrorism Financing: Due to the pseudonymous and decentralized nature of Bitcoin transactions, there are concerns about its potential use for illicit activities such as money laundering and terrorism financing. Regulators are tasked with implementing measures to prevent such activities while balancing the need for financial privacy.

3. Consumer Protection: The volatile nature of Bitcoin prices and the risk of hacks and scams in the cryptocurrency space pose challenges for consumer protection. Regulators need to ensure that investors are adequately informed and protected when engaging in Bitcoin transactions.

4. Taxation: The tax treatment of Bitcoin transactions varies widely across different jurisdictions, leading to complexity and confusion for taxpayers. Regulators need to provide clear guidance on how Bitcoin should be taxed to ensure compliance and fairness.

Opportunities:

1. Innovation and Financial Inclusion: Despite the challenges, Bitcoin presents opportunities for innovation in the financial sector. The underlying blockchain

technology has the potential to revolutionize traditional financial systems and increase financial inclusion for underserved populations.

2. Global Payments: Bitcoin's borderless nature allows for fast and low-cost cross-border payments, presenting opportunities for businesses and individuals to conduct international transactions more efficiently compared to traditional payment methods.

3. Regulatory Sandbox: Some regulators are exploring the concept of regulatory sandboxes, which allow fintech companies to test innovative products and services in a controlled environment. This provides an opportunity for regulators to understand the benefits and risks of Bitcoin and other cryptocurrencies before implementing broader regulatory frameworks.

4. Adoption of Blockchain Technology: Beyond Bitcoin, regulators are increasingly recognizing the potential of blockchain technology in various industries such as supply chain management, healthcare, and voting systems. By embracing blockchain innovation, regulators can foster economic growth and efficiency in these sectors.

In conclusion, the regulatory challenges and opportunities for Bitcoin are complex and evolving. Regulators need to strike a balance between fostering innovation and protecting consumers and financial stability. Collaborative efforts between policymakers, industry stakeholders, and the broader community are essential to navigate the regulatory landscape and unlock the full potential of Bitcoin and blockchain technology.

- Potential impact of Bitcoin on the global economy and financial systems
The potential impact of Bitcoin on the global economy and financial systems is a topic of much debate and speculation among economists, policymakers, and financial experts. As a decentralized digital currency, Bitcoin has the potential to

disrupt traditional financial systems and change the way we think about money and transactions. In this section, we will explore some of the key ways in which Bitcoin could impact the global economy and financial systems.

1. Financial Inclusion: One of the key potential impacts of Bitcoin is its ability to provide financial services to the unbanked and underbanked populations around the world. With Bitcoin, individuals can send and receive money without needing a traditional bank account, making it easier for people in developing countries to access financial services.

2. Reduced Transaction Costs: Bitcoin transactions are generally faster and cheaper than traditional bank transfers, especially for cross-border transactions. This could lead to lower transaction costs for businesses and individuals, potentially increasing economic efficiency and reducing barriers to trade.

3. Currency Competition: Bitcoin's growing popularity as a store of value and medium of exchange could challenge the dominance of traditional fiat currencies issued by governments. This could lead to increased competition among currencies, potentially leading to more stable and efficient monetary systems.

4. Financial Stability: Bitcoin's decentralized nature means that it is not subject to the control of any single government or institution. While this can be seen as a strength in terms of security and censorship resistance, it could also lead to increased financial instability if Bitcoin were to become a significant part of the global financial system.

5. Regulatory Challenges: The rise of Bitcoin presents challenges for regulators and policymakers, who must grapple with how to regulate a decentralized and global currency. Issues such as money laundering, tax evasion, and consumer protection are all areas of concern that will need to be addressed as Bitcoin continues to grow in popularity.

6. Investment Opportunities: The increasing acceptance of Bitcoin as an asset class has opened up new investment opportunities for individuals and institutions. This could lead to increased capital flows into the Bitcoin ecosystem, potentially driving up prices and creating new wealth creation opportunities.

Overall, the potential impact of Bitcoin on the global economy and financial systems is complex and multifaceted. While Bitcoin has the potential to bring about positive changes such as increased financial inclusion and reduced transaction costs, it also poses challenges in terms of regulatory oversight and financial stability. As Bitcoin continues to evolve and grow, it will be important for policymakers, businesses, and individuals to carefully consider the implications of its widespread adoption on the global economy.

Conclusion:

- Recap of key concepts covered in the book

Throughout the book "Basics of Bitcoin," several fundamental concepts have been covered to help readers understand the intricacies of Bitcoin and how it functions within the digital currency ecosystem. In this section, we will recap some of the key concepts discussed in the book:

1. Introduction to Bitcoin: The book begins with an introduction to Bitcoin, explaining its origins, purpose, and significance in the world of finance and technology. Readers learn about the creator of Bitcoin, Satoshi Nakamoto, and the vision behind the creation of this decentralized digital currency.

2. Blockchain Technology: The book delves into the concept of blockchain technology, which serves as the underlying technology behind Bitcoin. Readers gain an understanding of how transactions are recorded and verified on the blockchain, ensuring transparency, security, and immutability.

3. Mining and Consensus Mechanisms: The process of mining, where miners use

computational power to solve complex mathematical puzzles and validate transactions on the network, is explained in detail. The concept of consensus mechanisms, such as Proof of Work (PoW) and Proof of Stake (PoS), is also discussed to highlight how network consensus is achieved in the Bitcoin ecosystem.

4. Wallets and Addresses: Readers are introduced to the concept of Bitcoin wallets and addresses, which are essential for storing, sending, and receiving bitcoins. The different types of wallets, such as hardware wallets, software wallets, and paper wallets, are explained to help readers choose the most suitable option for their needs.

5. Security and Privacy: The book emphasizes the importance of security and privacy when dealing with Bitcoin. Readers learn about best practices for securing their wallets, protecting their private keys, and safeguarding their funds from potential threats such as hacking and phishing attacks.

6. Regulation and Adoption: The regulatory landscape surrounding Bitcoin and cryptocurrencies is discussed to provide readers with insights into the legal and regulatory challenges that the industry faces. The book also explores the growing adoption of Bitcoin by individuals, businesses, and institutions worldwide.

7. Future Trends and Developments: The book concludes by discussing future trends and developments in the world of Bitcoin, such as scalability solutions, improvements in transaction speed and cost, and the potential impact of central bank digital currencies (CBDCs) on the adoption of Bitcoin.

In summary, the book "Basics of Bitcoin" covers a wide range of key concepts that are essential for anyone looking to gain a comprehensive understanding of Bitcoin and its role in shaping the future of finance and technology. By mastering these concepts, readers can navigate the world of Bitcoin with confidence and make informed decisions regarding their involvement in the digital currency space.

- Encouragement for further exploration and learning about Bitcoin

Congratulations on completing the basics of Bitcoin! By now, you have gained a foundational understanding of this revolutionary technology and its implications for the future of finance and beyond. As you embark on your journey into the world of Bitcoin, here are some words of encouragement to fuel your curiosity and deepen your knowledge:

1. Embrace the Complexity: Bitcoin operates at the intersection of technology, economics, cryptography, and politics. While the basics provide a solid foundation, there is much more to discover and explore. Embrace the complexity of Bitcoin and be prepared to delve deeper into its intricacies.

2. Stay Curious: The world of Bitcoin is constantly evolving, with new developments, innovations, and debates emerging on a regular basis. Stay curious and remain open-minded to new ideas and perspectives. Engage with the Bitcoin community, attend conferences, read research papers, and follow industry experts on social media to stay informed.

3. Experiment and Learn by Doing: One of the best ways to deepen your understanding of Bitcoin is to get hands-on experience. Consider setting up a Bitcoin wallet, making a small transaction, or even running a Bitcoin node. By experimenting with the technology firsthand, you will gain practical insights that go beyond theoretical knowledge.

4. Explore Diverse Perspectives: Bitcoin is a diverse and vibrant ecosystem with a wide range of stakeholders, each with their own perspectives and motivations. Take the time to explore different viewpoints, from technical debates within the

developer community to philosophical discussions about the future of money. By engaging with a variety of perspectives, you will develop a more nuanced understanding of Bitcoin.

5. Keep Learning: The field of Bitcoin is vast and multifaceted, with numerous topics to explore, including scalability, privacy, security, governance, and more. Commit to lifelong learning and dedicate time to expanding your knowledge through books, podcasts, online courses, and other educational resources. Remember that learning about Bitcoin is a journey, not a destination.

In conclusion, the basics of Bitcoin are just the beginning of your exploration into this fascinating technology. By staying curious, embracing complexity, experimenting, exploring diverse perspectives, and committing to continuous learning, you will deepen your understanding of Bitcoin and contribute to the ongoing evolution of this groundbreaking innovation. Enjoy the journey ahead and may your exploration of Bitcoin be enlightening and rewarding.

- Final thoughts on the transformative potential of Bitcoin

In the book "Basics of Bitcoin," the transformative potential of Bitcoin is a topic of great importance and intrigue. As we delve deeper into the world of cryptocurrencies and blockchain technology, it becomes evident that Bitcoin has the power to revolutionize the way we think about money, finance, and even society as a whole.

Bitcoin, as the first decentralized digital currency, has sparked a paradigm shift in the way we perceive and interact with money. Its decentralized nature means that it is not controlled by any government or central authority, making it immune to manipulation or censorship. This gives individuals greater financial autonomy and control over their own wealth.

One of the most transformative aspects of Bitcoin is its ability to facilitate peer-to-peer transactions without the need for intermediaries such as banks or payment processors. This not only reduces transaction costs but also empowers individuals to transact directly with one another, bypassing traditional financial institutions.

Moreover, Bitcoin has the potential to provide financial services to the unbanked and underbanked populations around the world. By simply having access to the internet, individuals can participate in the global economy and send and receive payments securely and quickly, regardless of their location or socioeconomic status.

The underlying technology behind Bitcoin, known as blockchain, also has transformative potential beyond the realm of finance. Blockchain technology enables transparent and secure record-keeping, which can be applied to various industries such as supply chain management, healthcare, and voting systems.

However, it is important to acknowledge that the transformative potential of Bitcoin is not without challenges. Regulatory uncertainty, scalability issues, and environmental concerns related to energy consumption are some of the key hurdles that need to be addressed for Bitcoin to realize its full potential.

In conclusion, the transformative potential of Bitcoin is vast and far-reaching. As we continue to explore the possibilities offered by cryptocurrencies and blockchain technology, it is essential to consider the implications and opportunities that Bitcoin presents for reshaping our financial systems and society as a whole. It is a fascinating journey that is still unfolding, and only time will reveal the true extent of Bitcoin's impact on our world.

www.ingramcontent.com/pod-product-compliance
Lightning Source LLC
Chambersburg PA
CBHW030101230526
45471CB00003B/1206